THIS IS A LET'S-READ-AND-FIND-OUT SCIENCE BOOK

A BABY STARTS TO GROW

By Paul Showers

Illustrated by Rosalind Fry

Thomas Y. Crowell Company   New York

This Crowell Crocodile is one of the quality paperback editions
selected from Crowell's highly recommended:

―――― ∽ LET'S-READ-AND-FIND-OUT SCIENCE BOOKS ∽ ――――

Editors: Dr. Roma Gans, Professor Emeritus of Childhood Education, Teachers College, Columbia University
Dr. Franklyn M. Branley, Astronomer Emeritus and former Chairman of the American Museum—Hayden Planetarium

A Baby Starts to Grow
Bees and Beelines
Birds Eat and Eat and Eat
A Drop of Blood
Follow Your Nose
Hear Your Heart
High Sounds, Low Sounds
How a Seed Grows

How You Talk
It's Nesting Time
Ladybug, Ladybug, Fly Away Home
My Five Senses
My Visit to the Dinosaurs
Oxygen Keeps You Alive
Straight Hair, Curly Hair
The Sunlit Sea

A Tree Is a Plant
Use Your Brain
Water for Dinosaurs and You
What I Like About Toads
What Makes Day and Night
What the Moon Is Like
Why Frogs Are Wet
Your Skin and Mine

Copyright © 1969 by Paul Showers.
Illustrations copyright © 1969 by Rosalind Fry.
All rights reserved. Published simultaneously in Canada by Fitzhenry & Whiteside Limited, Toronto.
Manufactured in the United States of America.
L. C. Card 69-11827   ISBN 0-690-11325-0
2   3   4   5   6   7   8   9   10
CROWELL CROCODILE EDITION, 1972

A
LET'S-READ-AND-FIND-OUT SCIENCE BOOK

A BABY STARTS TO GROW

BY PAUL SHOWERS   Illustrated by Rosalind Fry

When a baby is born, he weighs about six pounds; he still has a lot of growing to do. A baby also grows before he is born. At first he is only one cell, not quite as big as the dot at the end of this sentence. This book tells how a baby develops from that single cell, how he is protected, and how he draws nourishment until he becomes strong enough to live outside his mother's body.

Paul Showers, co-author of *Before You Were a Baby*, has written this companion book about a baby's growth in clear, simple language a child can read to himself. The warm-hearted drawings are by Rosalind Fry.

LET'S
READ
AND
FIND
OUT →

When this baby was one day old, he weighed seven pounds.
He was twenty inches long from the top of his head to the tip of his heels.

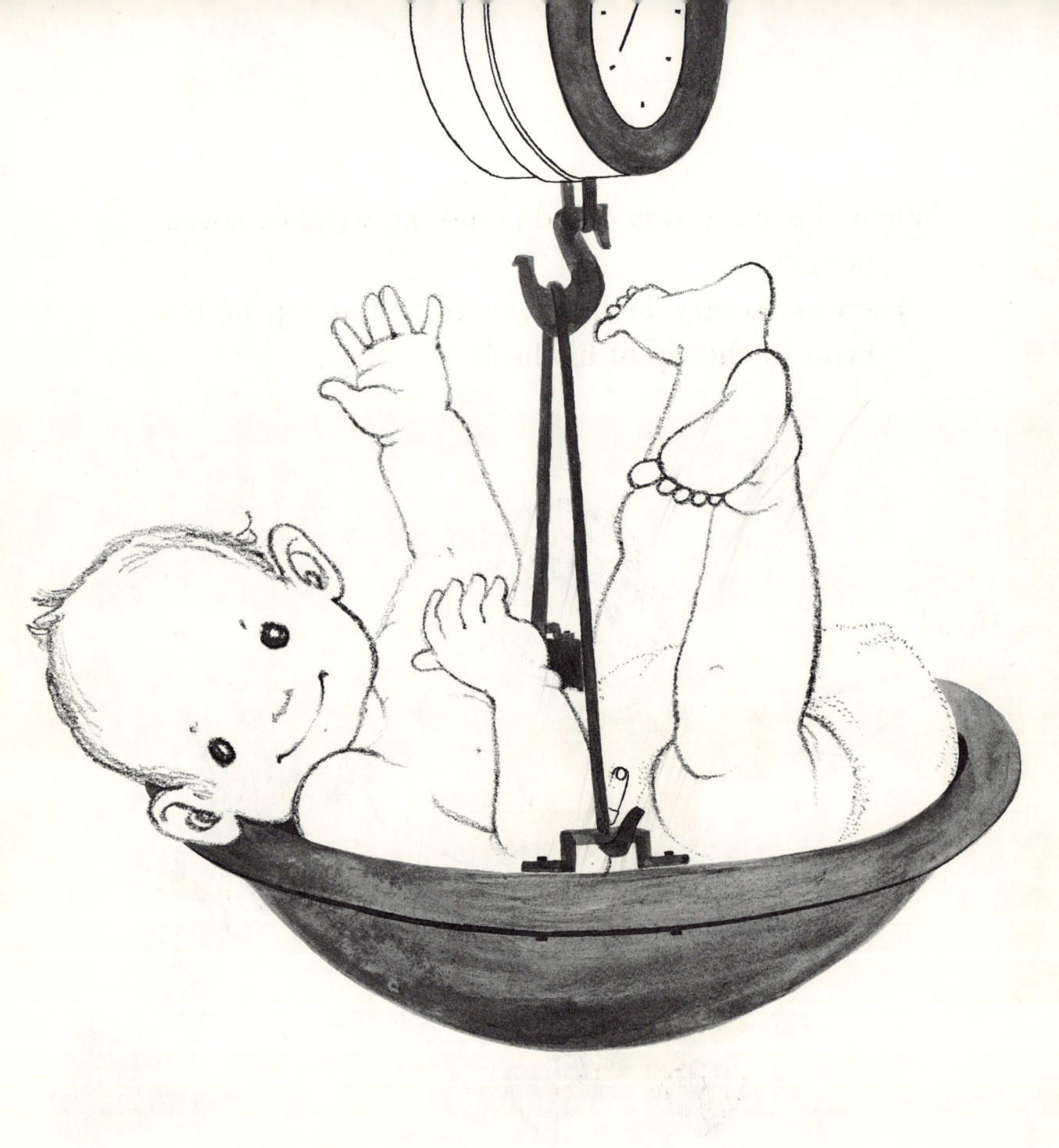

When he was one year old, he weighed twenty-one pounds.
He was thirty inches long, and everybody said:
"My, how he has grown!"

Babies grow before they are born, too.
> Before a baby is born, it grows inside its mother's body.
>
> It grows in a hollow place called the uterus, or womb.
>
> It grows a hundred million times bigger than it was when it began.

At first there is no baby at all.
   Then two very small cells join together.
   One is called the sperm. It comes from the father.
   The other is called the ovum. It is inside the mother.

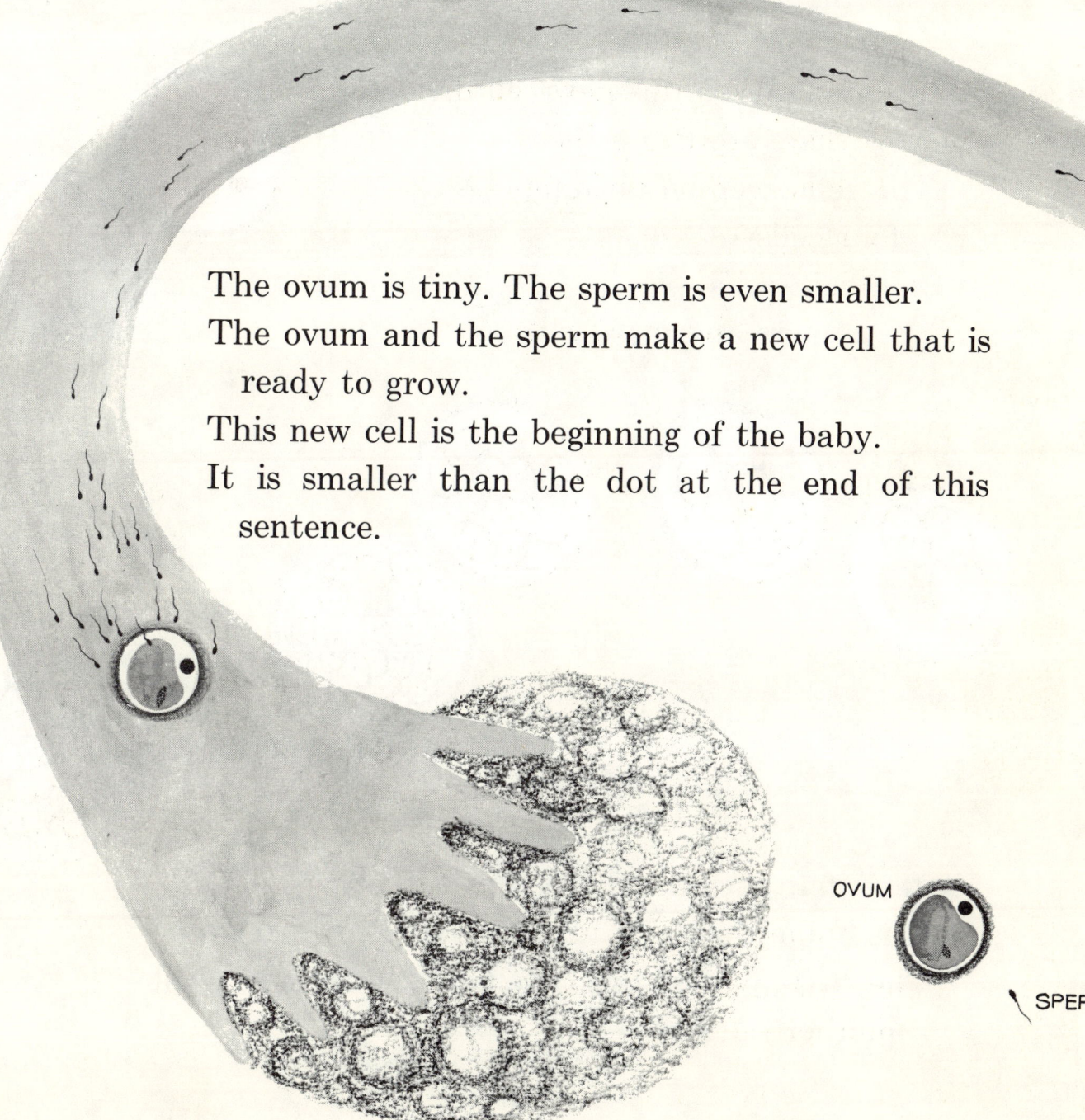

The ovum is tiny. The sperm is even smaller.
The ovum and the sperm make a new cell that is ready to grow.
This new cell is the beginning of the baby.
It is smaller than the dot at the end of this sentence.

After a day or so this new cell divides.
Now there are two cells.
The cells keep on dividing—
four cells—
eight cells—
more and more cells.

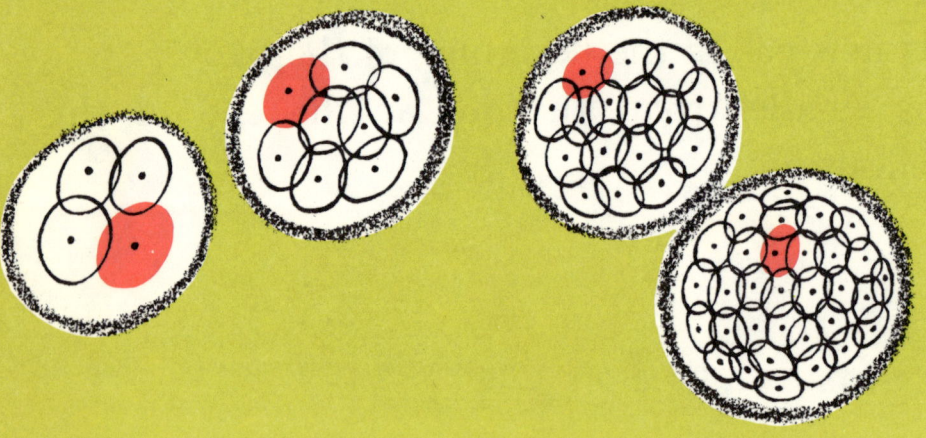

After a few days there is a tiny ball of cells.
It is hollow inside. The hollow is filled with water.
The little ball fastens itself to the inside of the
mother's uterus.

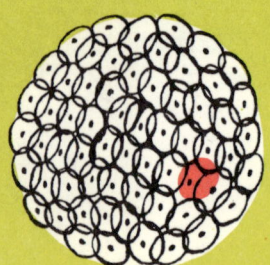

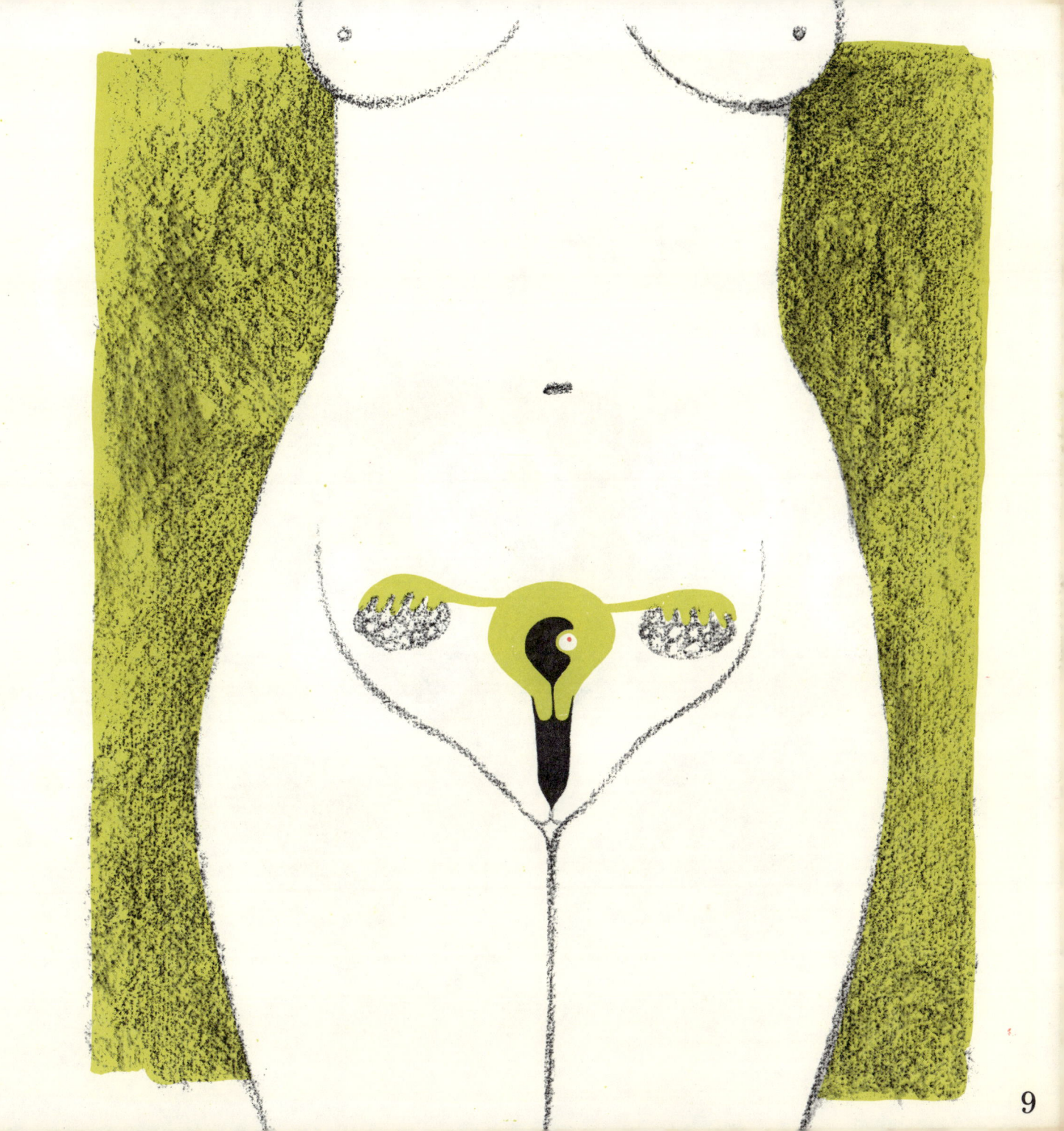

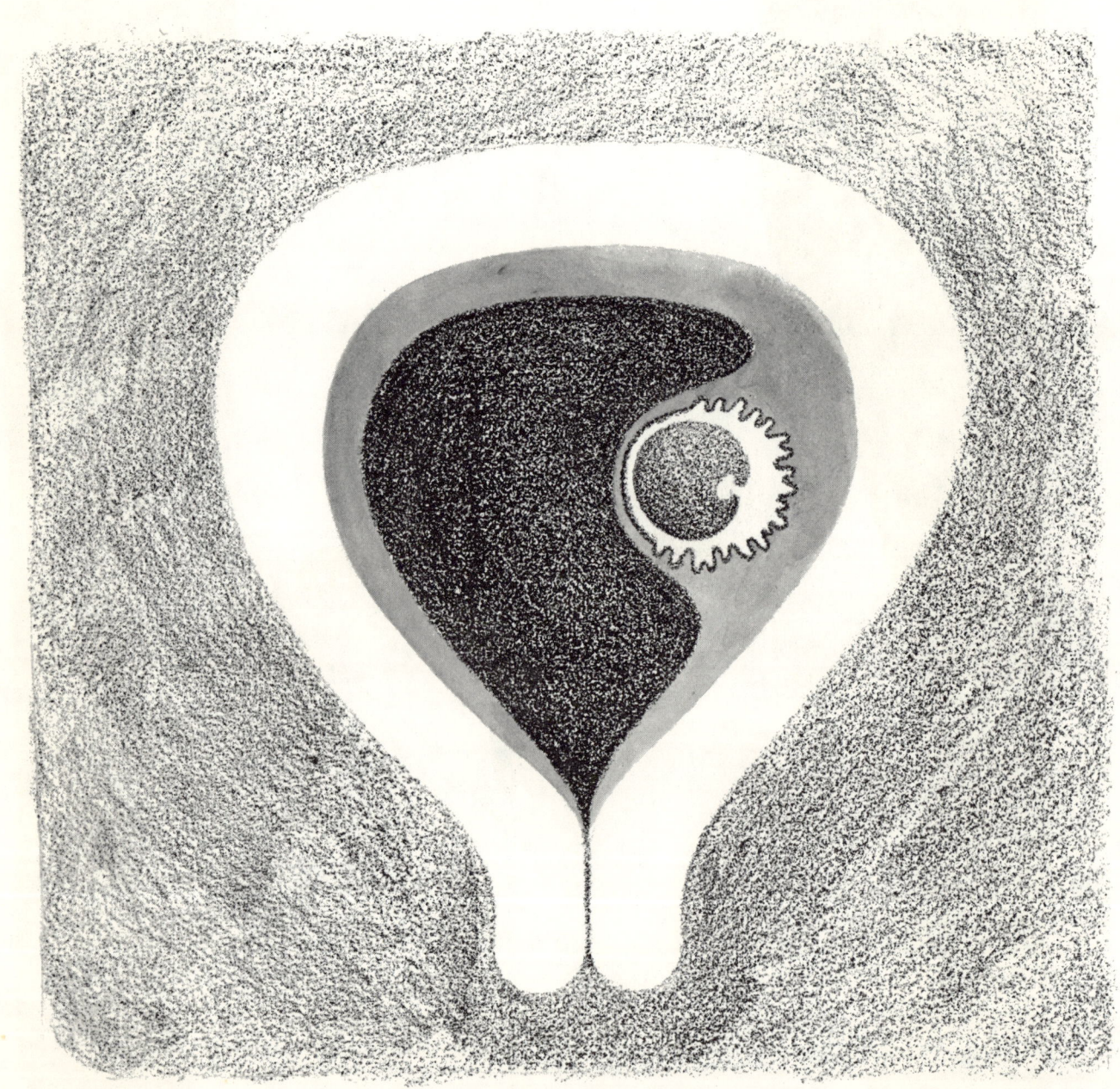

The ball is still very small, but it keeps growing.
   Thousands and thousands of new cells are made—
      millions and millions of new cells.
   The cells become different parts of the growing ball.

A thick stalk begins to grow in the water inside
      the ball.
   It grows out from one side of the ball.
   There is a lump at the end of the stalk.
   This lump is the baby.
   It doesn't look much like a baby.
   It looks like a very small bean.
   There is water all around it.

The baby is still very tiny.
   After four weeks the ball and the baby inside it are exactly this big.

But a baby grows fast.
 In five weeks it is almost twice as big as it was the week before.
 Now it has eyes and the beginnings of arms and legs.

In three more weeks fingers and toes begin to grow.
So do the ears.
Inside its body, the baby's heart is beating.
It moves the baby's blood through its body.
It moves the blood down into the stalk and back again.

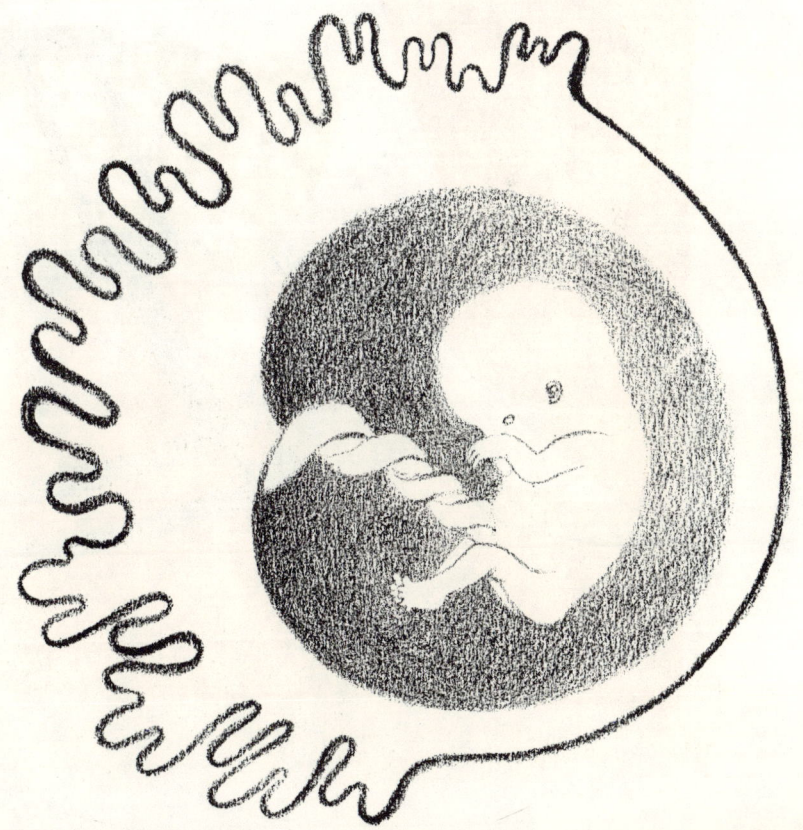

A baby needs food and oxygen to make it grow.
    We get oxygen from the air we breathe.
    The baby cannot eat or breathe inside the ball of water.
    It does not need to.
    Its mother eats and breathes for the baby.

When the mother eats, the food is digested in her stomach.
Then it goes into her blood.
When she breathes, oxygen from the air goes into her blood, too.

In the mother's uterus, her blood flows around the ball with the baby inside it.
The food and oxygen pass from the mother's blood through the side of the ball into the stalk.

Inside the stalk the baby's blood takes in the food and oxygen.
The blood carries food and oxygen up the stalk and to every part of the baby's body.

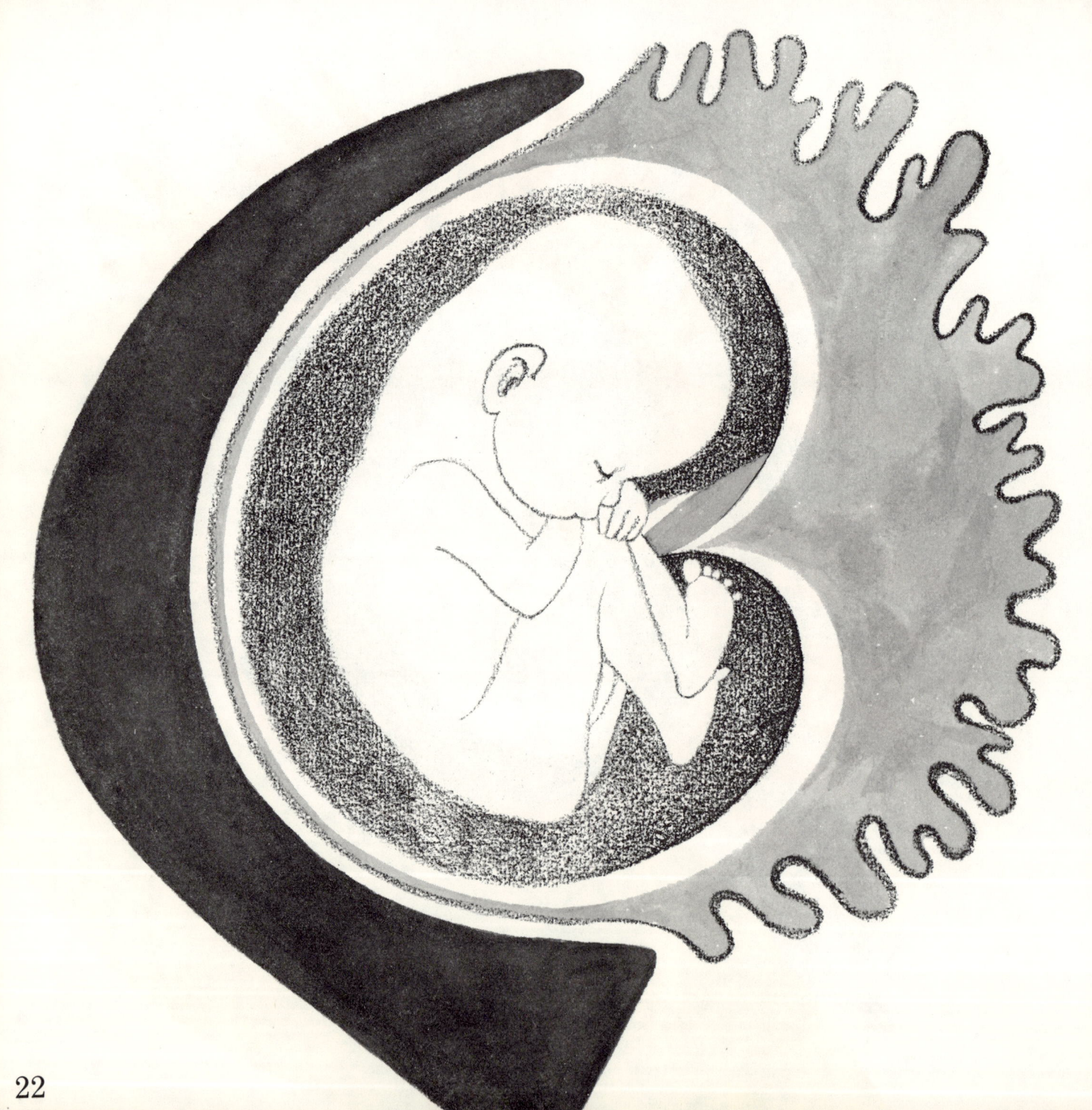

A baby grows very fast with the food and oxygen it takes from its mother.
After four months it is about eight inches long and it looks like a baby.
The ball full of water has stretched like a balloon.
The stalk has become a long, thick cord.
It is fastened to the middle of the baby.

The baby floats in the water inside the ball.
The water is like a cushion.
It keeps the baby from bumping its head or its knees or elbows.

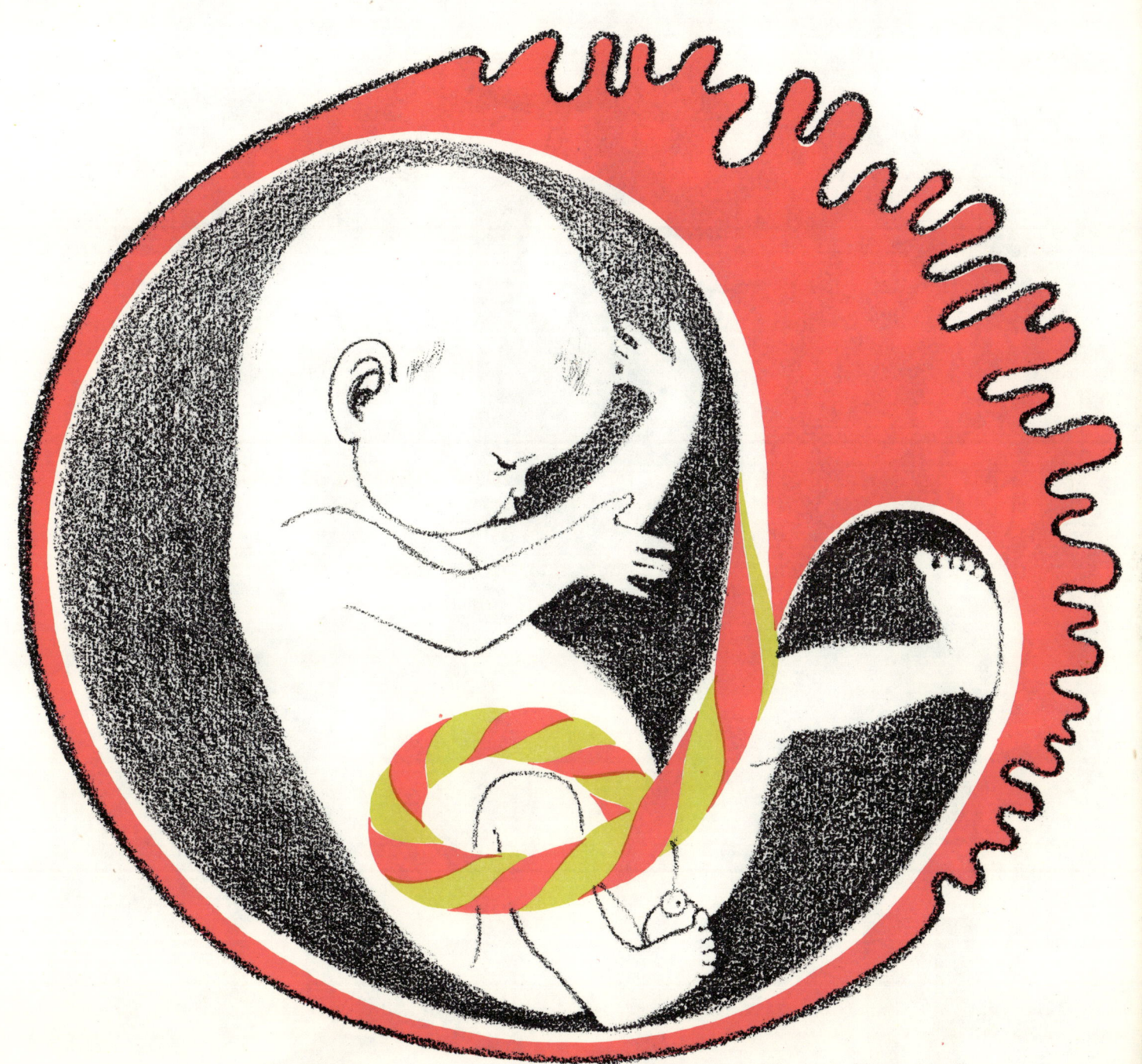

After five months the baby can move its hands and feet.
Its eyes are still shut. It can suck its thumb.
Sometimes its mother can feel it kicking.

As the weeks go by, the baby becomes bigger and stronger.
The ball of water grows bigger, too.
The ball pushes against the sides of the uterus.
The mother's stomach sticks out more and more.

At the end of nine months the baby is strong enough to live outside its mother's body.
Its eyes are ready to open and see.
Its ears are ready to hear.
The baby is ready to be born.

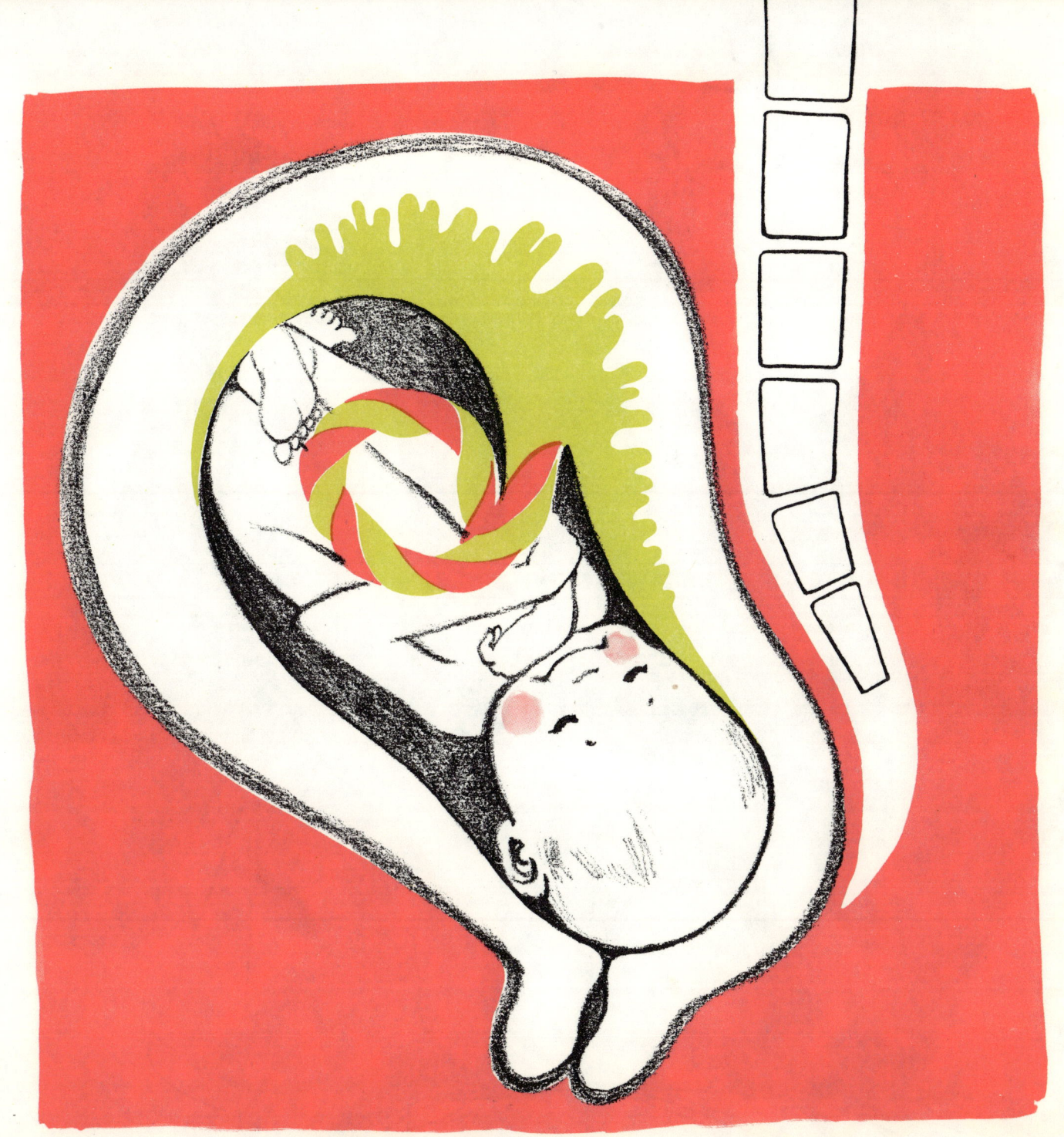

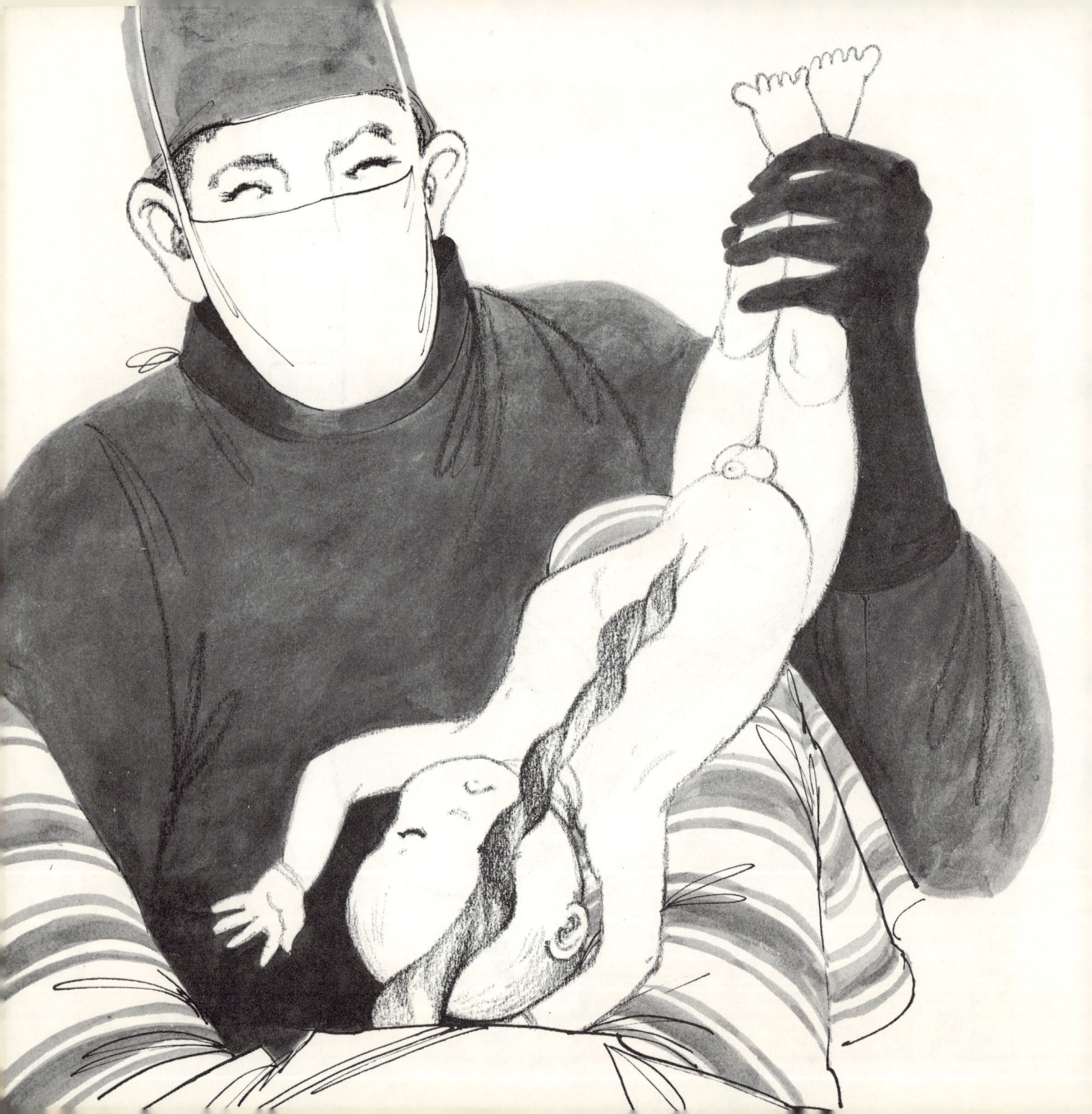

It comes slowly out of its mother's body into the world.
The cord is still fastened to the baby.

The doctor ties a string around the cord. He cuts the cord.
The place where the cord was fastened to the baby is the baby's belly button.

The baby doesn't need the cord any more.
   Its lungs are ready to breathe air.
   Its stomach is ready to digest food.
   The baby is ready to begin to live a life of its own.

ABOUT THE AUTHOR

Paul Showers is a newspaperman and writer. His first job was with the Detroit *Free Press;* later he worked on the New York *Herald Tribune.* During World War II he served in the Air Corps for a year, then joined the staff of *Yank,* the Army weekly. Since the war, with the exception of a brief stint with the New York *Sunday Mirror,* he has been on the staff of the Sunday *New York Times.*

Mr. Showers was born in Sunnyside, Washington, received his B.A. degree from the University of Michigan.

ABOUT THE ILLUSTRATOR

Rosalind Fry has lived in and traveled through most of her native Australia. Born in Brisbane, Queensland, she lived on a farm in Armidale, and then during World War II, journeyed 2,500 miles across the desert to Perth in Western Australia. She later moved to Melbourne and now lives in Sydney with her husband and five children.

A recipient of a diploma of illustration from Australia's National Art School, Miss Fry is a well-known illustrator. Her pictures have appeared in several books published both in the United States and abroad.